D1104116

Black Glass

by Margaret James

Photographs by Mark Billingsley

COLLECTOR BOOKS
P.O. Box 3009
Paducah, KY 42001

The current values in this book should be used only as a guide. They are not intended to set prices, which vary from one section of the country to another. Auction prices as well as dealer prices vary greatly and are affected by condition as well as demand. Neither the Author nor the Publisher assumes responsibility for any losses that might be incurred as a result of consulting this guide.

Additional copies of this book may be ordered from:

COLLECTOR BOOKS
P.O. Box 3009
Paducah, Kentucky 42001

@$5.95 Add $1.00 for postage and handling.

Copyright: Margaret James, 1981
ISBN: 0-89145-176-5

Printed by IMAGE GRAPHICS, Paducah, Kentucky

Dedication

I Dedicate This Book
To
My Husband Jerry

Acknowledgments

I would like to thank all the people who helped me in many different ways at one time or another. But I would like to especially thank the following:

ARLETTA, JERRI and LANCE; my children, for their constant support.

ARLINE WISE who helped me acquire some very special items.

BETTY NEWBOUND for her encouragement to get this book out of my dreams and down on paper.

Anyone having additional information that pertains to this book can write the author direct:

Margaret James
341 North 56 Street
Lincoln, Nebraska 68504

Foreword

Black Glass is a term for and also a description of a type of colored glass. Simply, it has the look of solid black. But there is a surprise in this glass. When it is held to the sun, or a strong light, color can be seen through it.

The most common color is deep purple which is called Black Amethyst. It can also show red, gold, grey, green, blue or grape. This latter color is a pinkish purple shade. As it appears to be opaque, it is sometimes called Black Milk Glass. It is very difficlt to see color through the thick items. This especially is true in solid glass animals.

Each glass house had is own formula for making black. Therefore, some glass will show a different color but that should not affect the price. Yet, the quality can. Also the availability of black from certain glass houses should be considered.

This glass was decorated in a variety of ways using enameling, corline, silver, gold and a heavy sterling silver deposit. It was also etched and sometimes given a satin finish. This was done either by the glass house or by firms which specialized only in decorating.

Some items have a combination of these decorations. Occasionally crystal, jade, colored or milk glass was combined with the black. There is a large variety of Art Glass using black as an accent. But this type falls into a different category.

Black glass has been made by many glass houses in America as well as in foreign countries. This makes it very difficult to identify. And the glass ranges from very old to brand new. A few of these companies went bankrupt, some failed to keep records or they were lost in fires. Also, the molds were loaned out or sold to other glass houses.

Sometimes a glass house will make up a special order for other companies, collector clubs, organizations, or department stores, etc. These places will then sell the items under their trade name which makes it very difficult to trace the original company.

Clues can be found in the many fine books written about the different varities of glass. Old magazine ads or glass catalogs are another source of information.

The asterisk in front of the pattern names are ones I gave to the item. This makes it easier to identify when advertising or ordering by mail.

I also powdered the raised patterns and etchings in order to show the designs in the pictures.

I have included a price guide but this is only to be used as a guide line. These suggestions are based on what I have seen at shows, flea markets, garage sales and in glass ads.

There are many combining factors which set a price on an item, such as demand, color, availability, condition and age. Some items are more abundant in one part of the country than in another. All of this will determine what the asking price will be. But the final word is what you are willing to pay.

This book was put together to show the beauty and large variety of black glass. There are many different and unusual items just waiting to be discovered.

Even though it is a challenge to identify, it is a joy to collect.

Table of Contents

Cambridge Glass Company

Console Bowl with orange and purple roses. White edging. 15¼" wide. Circa 1910-1915. $75.00-90.00

#300, 6" Candy Dish. Decorated with gold roses on lid and three leaf design inside bowl. Also gold on knob and feet. Circa 1930's. $45.00-50.00. #1236, 8" Ivy Ball. Keyhole crystal foot. Circa 1931 on. $30.00-35.00.

Handled Tray for sugar and creamer. Circa 1930's. $10.00-15.00. Base for Keg Set. Set includes colored keg, shot glasses, black round tray and base. Circa 1930's. $20.00-25.00.

"Calla Lily" Candlesticks #P-499. $30.00-35.00 pair.

#1191 Candlestick. Child kneeling on one knee holding up flared ribbed pot. Circa 1931. $50.00-55.00.

#3011/9, 3 oz. Cocktail. Black nude stem with crystal bowl and foot. Circa 1931. These have been reproduced by Imperial Glass Company. $40.00-42.00.

#782, 8" Vase with #736 etching. Circa 1930's. $40.00-45.00.

#3400/17, 12" Vase with gold encrusted etching #748 "Lorna". Circa 1930's. $60.00-65.00.

Duncan Miller Glass Company

#8, 12" Console Bowl with sterling silver deposit. Decorated by the Lotus Glass Company in their "Avalon" pattern, #57. Circa 1925. $75.00-80.00.

Candlesticks, 6¼" high. Sterling silver deposit in "Avalon" pattern #57. Circa 1925. $45.00-50.00 pair. Flat rim 11½" Console Vase with sterling silver deposit. Decorated by the Lotus Glass Company in their "Avalon" pattern #57. Circa 1925. $70.00-$75.00.

Salt Dip. "Three Leaf" pattern. Circa 1929. $10.00-15.00.
Shallow Bowl shown upside down. "Three Leaf" pattern. Gold
trim. Circa 1929. $18.00-20.00.

Fenton Art Glass Company

#6 Swan Candlesticks. 6½" high. Circa 1938. Rare.
$50.00-55.00 pair.

#6 Swan. 11½'' Bowl. Circa 1938. $65.00-75.00.

#1608, 10½'' Oval Bowl. Circa 1934. $80.00-85.00.

#1618 Elephant Flower Bowl. Very rare. Circa 1928. $220.00-225.00.

#1093 Three Toed Candleholders. Flat edge. Circa 1936. $20.00-25.00 pair. #1093 Crimped Bowl. Circa 1936. $20.00-25.00.

#9660 "Craftsman" Bell. Was never made in black. Was sample. 1979. $45.00-48.00. #1621 Dolphin Handled 6½" wavey edge plate or Bon-Bon. Circa 1934. $25.00-30.00.

#1532 Dolphin Handled Candy Dish. Circa 1928. $70.00-75.00. #835 Half-pound Candy Jar. Circa 1926. $35.00-40.00.

#3806 BW Salt and Pepper Shakers. January 1962 to July 1977. $10.00-15.00. #5156 Fish Vase. Made only in 1953. $50.00-55.00. #3872 Creative Candle Bowl. July 1968 to January 1975. This one is marked "Fenton" in a oval, Patent No. 3547569. $10.00-15.00.

#8251 "Mandarin" Vase. July 1968 to January 1969. $25.00-30.00. #8252 "Empress" Vase. July 1968 to January 1969. Both were Verly's molds. This one was called "Kuan Yin" or "Goddess" and renamed by Fenton. $25.00-30.00.

#5100 Praying Boy and Girl. Made from January 1973 to January 1974. $25.00-30.00. #5180 Wise Owl Decision Maker. January 1969 to July 1972. Band is missing. $15.00-17.00.

Fostoria Glass Company

#2436, 9" Lusters. Black stem and foot. Made in 1931. $38.00-40.00.

#2320, 11" Nappy Cupped "B". Made in the 1930's. $32.00-35.00.

#2419 Plate in the "Mayfair" pattern. With gold rings and edging. Circa 1930-1942. $5.00-6.00. #2350 After Dinner Cup and Saucer. With gold rings. Circa 1930-1942. $10.00-12.00.

#2419 Plate in "Mayfair" pattern. 1930-1942. $5.00-6.00.
Compote in "Mayfair" pattern. 5½" high. Circa 1930-1942.
$10.00-12.00. Sherbet with #36 "Poinsettia" etching. Circa
1924-1930. $10.00-12.00.

#2297, 10¼" Shallow Bowl. "A" Flared #53 pattern which is an
orange band. Circa 1930's. $15.00-20.00.

#2395½, 5" Candlesticks. Circa 1930's. $15.00-18.00 pair.
#2395, 10" Bowl. Circa 1930's. $15.00-20.00.

#2395, 3" Candlesticks. Circa 1930's. $15.00-18.00 pair.
#2324, 4" Candlesticks with gold trim. Circa 1930's.
$15.00-18.00 pair.

#2402, 9" Bowl. This also comes in a mint size. Circa 1930's. $9.00-12.00. #2375½ Tea Sugar and Creamer in the "Fairfax" pattern. Circa 1930-1942. $15.00-18.00 pair.

#2415 Combination Bowl. "Fern" design, plate etching #305 with gold edge. Circa 1929-1934. $30.00-35.00.

#2385, 8½'' Fan Vase. Unknown sterling silver design around top, middle and foot. Circa 1929-1930's. $60.00-65.00.

#2430 "Diadem" pattern, half-pound Candy Jar and cover. Gold trim. Circa 1929-1933. $15.00-18.00.

Greensburg Glass Works

#2 Elephant Ash Tray. 4" wide. This also comes in a 6¼" size. Circa 1930's. $13.00-15.00. #1 Dog Cigarette Box and Cover. Circa 1930's. $13.00-15.00. #1 Dog Ash Tray. 6¼" wide. This also comes in a 4" size. Circa 1930's. $13.00-15.00.

Hazel-Atlas Glass Company

"Floral Sterling" pattern on a sherbet. Circa 1930's. $3.00-4.00. Sherbet Plate in "Floral Sterling" pattern. Circa 1930's. $2.00-3.00. Plate in "Floral Sterling" pattern. 8" size. Circa 1930's. $3.00-4.00.

Hobb's Glass Company

"Windermere's Fan" Sugar Shaker. Hobb's Glass Company.
Circa 1890's. Rare. $120.00-125.00.

"Windermere's Fan" Covered sugar. Circa 1890's. Very rare.
$65.00-70.00.

Imperial Glass Company

Sherbet in "Diamond Quilted" pattern. Circa 1930's. $3.00-4.00. #3305 N, 5" Lily Bowl in "Diamond Block" pattern. Circa 1930's. $3.00-4.00. #330, 4¾" Handled Jelly Dish in "Diamond Block" pattern. Circa 1930's. $3.00-4.00.

Creamer in "Pillar Flute" pattern. Circa 1930's. $3.00-4.00. Two-handled 6¼" Pickle Dish in "Pillar Flute" pattern. Circa 1930's. $3.00-4.00. Bowl in "Pillar Flute" pattern. Circa 1930's. $3.00-4.00. Sugar in "Pillar Flute" pattern. Circa 1930's. $3.00-4.00.

Ruffled Edge Console Set. 12" wide. 3" high Candlesticks. Circa 1930's. $30.00-35.00 set.

Lancaster Glass Company

#901/4, 9½" Handled Tray with decoration #104D. Circa 1930's. $4.00-6.00. #901/4, 9½" Handled Tray with decoration #78. Circa 1930's. $4.00-6.00.

McKee Glass Company

Candlesticks. 4″ high. "Autumn" pattern. Circa 1934. $15.00-20.00 pair. Console Bowl. 7″ long. "Autumn" pattern. Circa 1934. $15.00-18.00.

"Tom and Jerry" Set. Silver writing. Marked "McKee". Circa 1930's. $70.00-75.00 set.

New Martinsville-Viking Glass Company

#10 "Queen Anne" Perfume Bottles. Has long stopper inside. Circa 1930's. $15.00-18.00 each. Flower Bowl with crystal frog. Circa 1940's. $18.00-20.00.

#679/1S, 12½" Oval Bowl with Swan Handle. Circa 1940's. $35.00-40.00. Swan Candlestick. Circa 1940's. $24.00-27.00.

Paden City Glass Manufacturing Company

"Peacock and Rose" 10" Vase. Circa 1928. $45.00-50.00.

L.E. Smith Glass Company

Scottish Terrier. 5" tall and 6" long with red collar, mouth and brown eyes. Circa 1930's. $18.00-20.00. Scottish Terrier. 3" tall and 3¾" long. No decoration. Circa 1930's. $14.00-15.00. Scottish Terrier. Miniature. 2½" long. Circa 1930's. $10.00-12.00.

Rearing Horse Bookend. Has mane all the way down to back. Marks for hoofs. Heavy ridges in tail. 8" high. Circa 1930's. $20.00-25.00. Mane goes halfway down neck. No marks on hoofs. Blurred ridges on tail. 7¾" high. These are from two different molds. This one is the later one. Circa 1930's. $20.00-25.00.

#2400 Two-handled Footed Fruit Bowl. Circa 1930's. $12.00-15.00. #2400 Two-handled Footed Bon-Bon. Circa 1930's. $8.00-10.00.

#1022 Three Footed Console Bowl. Circa 1930's. $12.00-15.00. Small Three Footed Console Bowl. Circa 1930's. $8.00-10.00.

#1/10 Fern Bowl. Circa 1930's. $10.00-12.00. #2/10 Fern Bowl with frog. Circa 1930's. $10.00-12.00.

Handled Plate with silver painted design. "Do-Si-Do"pattern. Circa 1930's. $8.00-10.00. #410 Salad Bowl. Circa 1930's. $10.00-12.00.

#404 Window Box. 8" long. This one has a double ridge at the top. Don't confuse it with #405/10. Sometimes called "Pan" and "Dancing Ladies". Circa 1930's. $13.00-15.00.

Hobnail Seven Piece Dresser Set. Black stoppers, lid and tray. Crystal bottoms. Circa 1932. $20.00-25.00.

#181 Handled Tumbler Tray. This was a Greensburg Glass Company item before Smith took over. Circa 1930's. $10.00-12.00.

Footed Bowl in "Lace Renaissance" pattern. Has scalloped edge. Circa 1928-1935. $20.00-25.00.

"Mt. Pleasant" pattern 8" Plate. This one has small points and no shield on backside. $5.00-8.00. "Mt. Pleasant" Cup and Saucer. Has sharp points and heavy scallops with shields on backside. Circa 1930's. $10.00-12.00. "Mt. Pleasant" 8" Plate. Has sharper points and heavy scallops with shields on backside. Circa 1930's. $5.00-8.00.

"Mt. Pleasant" pattern single Candlestick. Circa 1930's. $6.00-8.00. Three Footed 8" Plate in "Mt. Pleasant" pattern. Circa 1930's. $8.00-10.00. #600/4 Twin Candle Holder. Circa 1930's. $12.00-15.00.

#515 Footed Flared Bowl. Unknown sterling silver design by another company. Circa 1930's. $22.00-25.00. #515 Footed Cupped Bowl. Circa 1930's. $12.00-15.00.

Tray in "Mt. Pleasant" pattern. Tray also holds salt and pepper. Circa 1930's. $10.00-12.00. Creamer in "Mt. Pleasant" pattern. $6.00-8.00. Sugar in "Mt. Pleasant" pattern. $6.00-8.00. Handled Nut Tray in "Mt. Pleasant" pattern. $8.00-10.00.

Bean Pot with Lid. Silver "Daisy" design. 1930's. $30.00-35.00.
#327 Flared Cupped Bowl. Circa 1930's. $15.00-18.00.

#525 Bowls. The same bowl finished three different ways. Circa 1930's. $12.00-15.00.

United States Glass Company

#16273, 5" Aster Bowl. Circa 1930's. $13.00-15.00. #16254, 6" Iris Vase. Circa 1930's. $13.00-$15.00.

#9723, 10" Vase. Has pink and gold hand-painted flowers. Circa 1930's. $15.00-18.00. Satin-finish Vase with a gold cattail design. Also gold on rim and foot. Circa 1930's. $15.00-20.00. #16261, 8½" Satin-finish Vase. Circa 1930's. $15.00-20.00. #16270, 7½" Bud Vase. Circa 1930's. $8.00-10.00.

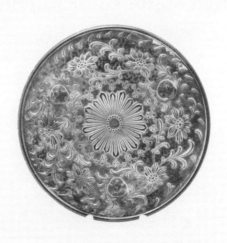

"Shaggy Daisy" Cake Plate. The white spots on the rim are from the plastic holder. Circa 1930's. $16.00-18.00.

#8127 Satin-finish "Elysium" pattern Bulb Box. 9½" long. Circa 1926. $35.00-40.00.

Black satin "Chessie Cat." 11" high. Circa 1929-1941.
$90.00-100.00.

#16255, 8" "Poppy" Vase. Red and green flowers. Satin finish.
Circa 1930's. $25.00-30.00.

Westmoreland Glass Company

Chicken Sherbet. Head and tail in satin finish. Circa 1930's.
$16.00-18.00.

#1049 Shell Compote. 6" high. Has matching candlesticks. Circa 1950's. $45.00-50.00.

Turtle Cigarette Box. Circa 1948. $35.00-38.00. Matching Ash Trays. $5.00-8.00.

*"Pam" Console Set. Silver painted flowers on bowl and candlesticks. Circa 1930's. $35.00-40.00 set.

Czechoslovakia

Fourteen Piece Bathroom Set. Colorful enameled *"Castle Scene." Ground stoppers with matching numbers on lids and bottles. Pontil on bottoms. Marked "Czechoslovakia." Rare. Circa 1920. $125.00-130.00 set.

England

*"Staggered Block" Match Holder. 3½". Mark is numbers and letters in a diamond. This is Sowerby's Ellison Glass Works; Gateshead-on-Tyne in Northeast England, mark. March 7, 1876. $40.00-45.00. *"Rippled Wave" Match Holder. 3¼". English mark. June 21, 1872. $40.00-45.00. *"Percy" Compote. 3¾". English mark. January 13, 1877. $30.00-35.00.

Miscellaneous
Candlesticks

*"Garrett" #177, 8½" high Candlesticks. This pair has a bubble inside each well and looks to be floating. There are other items which show a mirror-like object inside but this is due to light reflection. Paden City Glass Company. Circa 1930's. $25.00-28.00 pair. *"Tracy" Candlesticks. 7" high. Cambridge Glass Company. $25.00-28.00 pair.

*"Kiri" Candlesticks. 8½" high. Maker unknown. Circa 1930's. $20.00-22.00 pair. *"Jed" Candlesticks. 7" high. Maker unknown. Circa 1930's. $20.00-22.00 pair.

*"Waffer" Candlesticks. 7" high. Maker unknown. Circa 1930's. $20.00-22.00 pair. *"Licorice Life Saver" Candlesticks. 5¾" high. Maker unknown. $22.00-25.00 pair.

"Zaricar" Candlestick. 9" high. Central Glass Works. Circa 1924. $14.00-16.00. *"Rebel" Candlestick. 8½" high. Cambridge Glass Company. Circa 1930's. $20.00-22.00. *"Wrap Around" #1933 Candlestick. 6½" high. Marked "Westmoreland." Circa 1947. $15.00-18.00. *"Echo" #116, 7" Candlestick. Paden City Glass Company. Also made in 10" size. $12.00-15.00.

*"Yorkie" #1002 Candlesticks. 3" high. Greensburg Glass Works. Circa 1930's. $14.00-16.00 pair. *"Ellen" Candlesticks. 3¼" high. Orange enameled flowers and green leaves. Maker unknown. Circa 1930's. $18.00-20.00 pair. *"Flower Cup" Candlesticks. Looks like upside-down flower. Can be used either way. Maker unknown. Circa 1930's. $15.00-17.00 pair.

*"Avis" Candlesticks. Square corners turn down slightly. Maker unknown. $10.00-12.00 pair. "Triad" Candlesticks. Triangle shape. Maker unknown. $14.00-16.00 pair. *"Pete and Repete" Candlesticks. 2½" high. The last one's base is thicker and the stem is shorter. Circa 1930's. $5.00-7.00 each.

*"Garth" Black Satin Candlesticks. 3½" high. Gold rim and flowers on base. United States Glass Company. $15.00-20.00 pair. *"Dilly" #1402, 3½" high Candlestick. Greensburg Glass Works. Circa 1920's. $4.00-6.00. *"Hot Shot" Handled Candlestick. 4" high. Federal Glass Company. Circa 1930's. $8.00-10.00.

*"Proud" #2324, 3½" Candlestick. 1½" candle hole. Fostoria Glass Company. $8.00-10.00. *"Flying Saucer" Candlestick. 2" high. 6" round. Maker unknown. $8.00-10.00. *"Lucy" Candlestick. Holder in center of deep well. Six columns around outside. $10.00-12.00. *"Flossie" Candlestick. Unusual feel to glass but not satin finish. Maker unknown. $10.00-12.00. *"Dally" Candlestick. 4" high. Indiana Glass Company. Circa 1929. $8.00-10.00.

Northwood Bushel Basket. Marked "N" in a circle. $45.00-50.00. Handled Basket. 6¼" high. $20.00-25.00. Two Handled Basket. Imperial Glass Company. $25.00-30.00.

#4 Oval Bon-Bon. *"Pond Lily and Leaf" pattern. Fenton Art Glass Company. Circa 1915. $30.00-35.00. #1192 Bowl with Blackberry interior. Fenton Art Glass Company. Circa 1911. $40.00-45.00.

"Chrysanthemum and Windmill" Three-Toed Bowl. Fenton Art Glass Company. Circa 1908-1914. Rare. $95.00-100.00.

Covered Dishes

Hen on Nest. Basketweave base. Turned white opalescent head. Worn red paint on comb. Traces of gold at back of head. Feather detail on neck. Straw-look rim is 5 1/8" long and 4" wide. Circa 1900's. $100.00-110.00. Rooster top with beak missing. Straight white head. Dark lavender-black color. Slight slag look in underside but not marble look. Westmoreland Glass Company. $45.00-50.00. Hen on Nest. Diamond weave base. Milk white turned head. Worn red paint on comb. Straight lines on neck. Plain rim is 5 3/8" long and 4¼" wide. Westmoreland Glass Company. Circa 1900's. $100.00-110.00.

53

Covered Swan Dish. Westmoreland Glass Company. Circa 1950's. $100.00-110.00. Pomade Bear. Sandwich Glass Company. 4'' high. Muzzle on face. Circa 1850-1880. $100.00-110.00. Robin on Nest. Westmoreland Glass Company. Circa 1950's. $100.00-110.00.

Two-piece Elephant. Good eye, tail and wrinkle detail. Co-op Flint Glass Company. Circa 1920-30's. $65.00-70.00. Two-piece Elephant. Painted eye and white tusks. Also red and yellow tasseled blanket. Lid has place for sponge and pencils or for ashtray and cigarettes. Circa 1920-1930's. $70.00-75.00.

Two-piece Standing Rooster. 8½" high. Dark red painted comb. Marked "Westmoreland" inside rooster head. Circa 1950's. $75.00-80.00.

Lamps

"Crown" Lamp. 10" high. Black foot with crystal font. Advertised in November 1897 and called "Crystal Lamps." Also comes in 5¼" size. Dalzell, Gilmore and Leighton Company of Findlay, Ohio. $85.00-90.00. "Sheldon Swirl" Lamp. Crystal swirled font with black leaf patterned foot. Circa 1890-1900. $90.00-100.00.

*"Bust of Lady" Lamp. Font is "Triple Peg and Loop" with cut flowers and leaves on top half. Patented February 29, 1876. Atterbury and Company. $120.00-125.00. Lamp. Font is "Bullseye, Fleur-De-Lis and Heart" pattern. Circa 1860's. $100.00-110.00.

Houze Lamp. 9¾" high. Circa 1930's. $15.00-20.00. Lamp with "Nymph" pattern on base. Circa 1930's. $15.00-20.00. "Scottie" Lamp. Dog is the L.E. Smith Scottie. Shade is frosted with a cream color paint on the inside and a black Scottie decoration. Circa 1930's. $45.00-50.00.

Two-piece Lamp. 13¼" high. Metal lining inside base. $500.00-550.00.

Lamp. 9½'' high with pontil on bottom. Enameled orange and white flowers on font and foot. Three Feather tiny chimmey. Correct holder but wrong shade. Circa late 1800's. $100.00-110.00.

Miniature Animals

Bridge Dog. Cambridge Glass Company. Circa 1930's. $10.00-12.00. Cat with matte finish. Gold ribbon around neck. Rhinestone eyes. 2¾" high. $15.00-20.00. Bulldog with satin finish. Brown collar. Painted red and white eyes. 2½" high. Not Westmoreland. $15.00-20.00.

St. Nick. 1". Painted features. White beard and red cap. $22.00-25.00. Stick Pin. Size of a pea. Face with curly hair, red mouth, black and white eyes. $2.00-3.00. Monkey. 1 1/8". Metal collar. Rhinestone eyes. $25.00-30.00. Bulldog. 1". Chain and metal collar with glass ball. Rhinestone eyes. $18.00-20.00. Bulldog. 1". Metal collar with gold ball. Glass eyes. $18.00-20.00. Sitting Cat. 7/8". Rhinestone eyes. Collar marked "Made in Czechoslovak" with amethyst ball. $18.00-20.00.

Reclining Cats. Marked "C" in a circle with tiny "s".
Trademark of L.E. Smith. These are not from the same mold.
Circa 1930's. $14.00-16.00. Elephants. Marked "C" in a circle
with tiny "s". These are not from the same mold. L.E. Smith
Glass Company. Circa 1930's. $14.00-16.00.

Cow. Marked "C" in a circle. L.E. Smith Glass Company. Circa
1930's. $14.00-16.00. Rooster. Marked "C" in a circle. L.E.
Smith. Circa 1930's. $14.00-16.00. Goose. L.E. Smith Glass
Company. Circa 1930's. $14.00-16.00. Rearing Horse. Marked
"C" in circle. L.E. Smith. Circa 1930's. $14.00-16.00. Squirrel
holding nut. L.E. Smith Glass Company. Circa 1930's.
$14.00-16.00.

Penguin. 2" high. White belly and feet. Red snoot. Black and white eyes. $3.00-4.00. Duck. ¾" high. Orange eyes, beak and wings. $3.00-4.00. Horse. White on chest. Paper label, "Exco, Japan". $5.00-6.00. Duck. 1" high. $3.00-4.00. Dog. White on chest. "Made in Occupied Japan" paper label. $4.00-5.00.

Standing Fat Cat. $1.00-1.25. Standing Skinny Cat. $1.00-1.25. Cat reclining with red slag ball. 3" long. $1.50-2.00. Cat reclining with red slag ball. 2½" long. $1.50-2.00. Sitting Skinny Cat. $1.00-1.25. Sitting Fat Cat. $1.00-1.25.

Bird. Black body and white wings. Tan feet and beak. "Made in China" paper label. $2.00-3.00. Camel. Covered with silver-gray coating. $3.00-4.00. Penguin. Covered with silver-gray coating. Pearl covered stomach. $3.00-4.00.

Mugs

*"Profile" Mug. Raised side view of head in dotted circle. Laurel leaves cross under head. Pattern on both sides. Late 1800's. $35.00-40.00. *"Feathered Friend" Toy Mug. Barber pole design on handle. Late 1800's. $32.00-35.00.

Novelties

Pipe. 5¾" long. Rests on three legs. Gold trim. $8.00-10.00.
Frying Pan. Two pouring spouts. 5¼" wide. Gold rim.
$10.00-12.00. Bath Tub. Gold rim. Lettering says "Souvenir of
Council Bluffs Iowa". $10.00-12.00. Canoe. Gold rim. 6" long.
Lettering says "Souvenir of Mankato, Minn." $10.00-12.00.

Top Hat. English hobnail. $8.00-10.00. Coal Bucket. Wire han-
dle. $8.00-10.00. Oaken Bucket. Wire handle. $8.00-10.00.
Witches Pot. Three feet. $8.00-10.00.

Plates

"Keyhole Border" Plate. $10.00-15.00. "Ring and Dot Border"
Plate. $10.00-15.00. "Gothic Border" Plate. $10.00-15.00.

"Square S Border" Plate. 9¼". $18.00-25.00. "Club and Shell Border" Plate. 9¼". $18.00-25.00.

"Triangle S Border" Plate. $20.00-30.00. "Heart Border" Plate. 8". $20.00-30.00.

A variant of the "Backward C Square Border" Plate. $20.00-30.00. "Leaf and Scroll Square Edge Border" Plate. $20.00-30.00.

"Wicket Border" Plate. 9¼". Atterbury. Circa 1880's. $18.00-25.00. "Pinwheel Border" Plate. 8¼". $18.00-25.00.

"Stanchion Border" Plate. Challinor, Taylor and Company. $25.00-30.00. "Three Owls" Plate. Marked "Westmoreland". $25.00-30.00.

"For-Get-Me-Not Border" Plate. White enameled grazing deer. Very thick and heavy. Marked "Westmoreland". $25.00-30.00. "For-Get-Me-Not Border" Plate. White enameled running stag. Very thin and light. Old. $25.00-30.00.

"For-Get-Me-Not Border" Plate. White enameled girl swinging. Very thick and heavy. 1957 on. Westmoreland. $25.00-30.00. "For-Get-Me-Not Border" Plate. White enameled boy fishing. 1957 on. Very thick and heavy. Westmoreland. $25.00-30.00.

"For-Get-Me-Not Border" Plate. White enameled girl playing with dog. Very thick and heavy. Signed by artist C.F. Steeley 1970. Westmoreland. $25.00-30.00. "For-Get-Me-Not Border" Plate. White enameled boy with rake and dog. Very thick and heavy. Marked "Westmoreland". 1957 on. $25.00-30.00.

"For-Get-Me-Not Border" Plate. White enameled boy skating with dog. Signed by artist, "S. Mitler 1975". Marked "Westmoreland". $25.00-30.00 "For-Get-Me-Not Border" Plate. White enameled girl skating pulling dog on sled. Very thick and heavy. Marked "Westmoreland". 1957 on. $25.00-30.00.

Powder Boxes

*"Simple Simon" Powder Box. Sterling silver deposit on lid. Circa 1930's. $10.00-15.00. *"Pretty Polly" Octagon Powder Box. With colorful coraline parrot and flowers on lid. Circa 1930's. $10.00-15.00. *"Ruth" Powder Box with pattern on lid and under base. Circa 1930's. $10.00-15.00.

*"Nymph" Powder Box. Lid was used for lamp base also. Circa 1930's. $10.00-15.00. *"Clown Head" Powder Box. Gold trim on base and lid. Clown finial on lid. Circa 1930's. $45.00-47.00. "Hobnail" Powder Box. With variations of hobnails. Circa 1930-1940's. $10.00-15.00.

Salt Dips

*"Pee Wee" Salt Dip. Circa 1930's. $8.00-10.00. "Lotus" Salt Dip. Westmoreland Glass Company. Circa 1930's $9.00-10.00. *"Tiny Tot" Salt Dip. Circa 1930's. $8.00-10.00. "Three Leaf" Salt Dip. Duncan Miller Glass Company. Circa 1930's. $8.00-10.00.

Shoes

Boot with spur. $35.00-40.00. Ladies Shoe. Bow at front with cube heel. English mark. Used between January 1887 and January 1888. $55.00-60.00.

Spice Holders

*"Squatty" Spice Holders. 3". Metal lids. Circa 1930's. $10.00-12.00 each. "Colonial" Spice Holders with metal shaker tops. 4¼". Made by Sneath Company, Hartford City, Indiana. Were sold in sets of five and seven. Circa 1930's. $10.00-12.00 each.

Salt & Pepper Shakers

Salt and Pepper Shakers. Hazel Atlas Glass Company. Circa 1930's. $10.00-14.00 pair. Handled Shaker. "Flo" pattern. $7.00-8.00.

Swans

Large Swan. 9¼". Marked "C" in a triangle. Cambridge Glass Company. $90.00-100.00. Small Swan. 3¾". Marked "C" in a triangle. Cambridge Glass Company. $45.00-50.00. Medium Swan. 6½". Marked "C" in a triangle. Cambridge Glass Company. $65.00-75.00.

Large Swan trimmed in silver. "Kimberly" pattern. L.E. Smith Glass Company. Circa 1930's. $35.00-45.00. #974/1S, 5" Dish with Swan Handle. Black body and crystal neck. Viking Glass Company. Circa 1940-1960. $15.00-20.00.

*"Elegant" Swan. Wing feathers are very detailed. A bit shorter and back opening is a little wider than the Fenton swan. Not Imperial. $20.00-25.00. "Fenton" Swan. Flower-like feathers on wing. Both swans have dots half way down their necks. Circa 1930's. $20.00-25.00.

Toothpicks

*"Half Scroll" Toothpick. Tiny scroll and beads on rim. 1¾".
$15.00-18.00. "Bee's on a Basket" Toothpick. Originally made
as a match holder. $60.00-65.00. *"Tasseled Fan" Toothpick.
"Button and Daisy" design with four tassels on base.
$25.00-30.00. *"Pot Belly" Toothpick. 2½". Blue enameled
flowers and silver trim. $25.00-27.00.

Vases

"Mary Gregory" Vase. 7½". Gold rim. Original idea came
from the firm of Holm which decorated glass in Jablavec,
Bohemia between 1850-1890. Mary Gregory worked for the
Sandwich Glass Company in the late 1800's. $65.00-70.00.
Square Vase. 8½". Colorful enameled stork scene on front.
Flowers on three sides. Gold trim on rim. Late 1800's.
$30.00-35.00. Vase with fluted gold trimmed rim. 6¼". White
enameled flowers and pontil on bottom. Circa late 1800's.
$20.00-22.00.

73

Vase with colorful enameled flowers and gold trim on fluted rim. Pontil on bottom. Late 1800's. $30.00-35.00. Vase with enameled blue and white flowers and yellow leaf. Gold trim on fluted rim and pontil on bottom. 9¾''. Late 1800's. $40.00-45.00. Vase with enameled white flowers and pontil on bottom. Bristal style vases like these three were made in the Strausbridge, England area from the 1870's on as well as in America. $50.00-55.00. Vase with colorful enameled design. 9¾'' high. Circa 1920-1930's. $12.00-15.00.

Victorian Items

Large dish with lid. "Versailles" pattern. Raised roses with green leaves and gold trim. Number "184" on bottom. Circa late 1800's. $40.00-45.00. Pin Dish with number "25" inside lid. Gold painted raised design. Late 1800's. $10.00-15.00.

*"Margaret's Toilet Set". Two scent bottles and jar with ground stoppers and pontils on bottom. 5½". Enameled green, white and cream flowers. Silver plated holder is 15½". Marked "Middletown Plate Company". Circa 1866-1899. $125.00-130.00 set.

Vase with enameled orange and yellow flowers and yellow
butterfly. 11¼" high. Circa 1880-1890's. $50.00-55.00. Luster
with seven cut glass prisms, each 7" long. 11¾". White flowers
in a gold design. Circa 1880-1900. $70.00-75.00.

Unknown Mixture

*"Gee Whiz" Cheese and Cracker Set. Gold pattern on plate
and gold trim on cheese sherbet. Circa 1930's. $25.00-30.00.

*"Arletta" Coffee Cup. Circa 1930's. $3.00-4.00. *"Dotted Band" Coffee Cup. Circa 1930's. $3.00-4.00. *"Jerri'" Coffee Cup. Circa 1930's. $3.00-4.00.

*"Show Time" 13" Bowl with gold encrusted design on rim. Circa 1930's. $25.00-30.00. Handled Plate. 11" wide. Gold encrusted * "Gallent Lance" design on rim but the rest of etching doesn't have the gold. Circa 1930's. $25.00-30.00.

Cigarette Holder #2349. Fostoria Glass Company. Circa 1920-1929. $7.00-9.00. *"Perky" Pedestal. 5" high. $4.00-5.00. Pistol. Circa 1926. Westmoreland Glass Company. Reproduced in 1973. $8.00-10.00. *"Little Squirt" Shot Glass. Plain. 1½ oz. $3.00-3.50. *"Arched Squirt" Shot Glass. Arch design around bottom. 1½ oz. $3.00-3.50.

Pattern Index